Science Matters
EXPLORING SPACE

Pat York

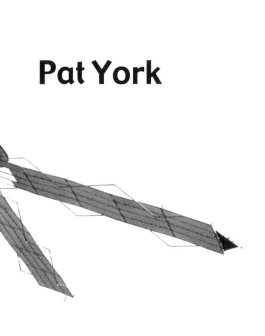

WEIGL PUBLISHERS INC.

Published by Weigl Publishers Inc.
123 South Broad Street, Box 227
Mankato, MN USA 56002
Web site: www.weigl.com

Library of Congress Cataloging-in-Publication Data

York, Pat, 1949-
  Exploring space / Pat York.
       v. cm. -- (Science matters)
Includes index.
Contents: Getting to know space -- Looking up -- Moonwalk -- Next stop, Mars! -- Map of our solar system -- The International Space Station -- Hubble searches space -- Future in the sky -- Surfing our solar system -- Science in action -- What have you learned?
  ISBN 1-59036-085-0 (Library Bound : alk. paper)
  1. Astronautics--Juvenile literature. 2. Outer space--Exploration--Juvenile literature. [1. Astronautics. 2. Outer space--Exploration.] I. Title. II. Series.
  TL789 .Y67 2003
  629.4--dc21
                              2002013852

Printed in the United States of America
1 2 3 4 5 6 7 8 9 0 06 05 04 03 02

Project Coordinator Jennifer Nault **Design** Terry Paulhus
Copy Editor Tina Schwartzenberger **Layout** Bryan Pezzi
Photo Researcher Tina Schwartzenberger

Photograph Credits
Every reasonable effort has been made to trace ownership and to obtain permission to reprint copyright material. The publishers would be pleased to have any errors or omissions brought to their attention so that they may be corrected in subsequent printings.

Cover: Astronaut from NASA
Archive Photos: page 7; Warren Clark: pages 12–13; COMSTOCK, Inc.: pages 1, 6, 14, 15, 16, 18, 19; Bettmann/CORBIS/MAGMA: pages 9, 17; Corel Corporation: pages 3T, 3B, 21, 23T; Digital Vision: pages 3M, 11, 22T, 23M, 23B; NASA: pages 4, 8, 10; PhotoDisc, Inc.: page 22B.

Contents

Studying Space

Humans have been exploring their world for thousands of years. People love to discover and learn about new places. Some of today's explorers are making exciting new discoveries in space.

Many objects are found in the **universe**. These include **asteroids**, planets, moons, comets, and stars. Astronomers are scientists who study the objects in space. People who travel to space to learn about it are called astronauts.

■ The *Hubble Space **Telescope*** circles Earth. It has three cameras that photograph objects in space.

Space Facts

Did you know that the universe is believed to be 15 billion years old? Read on to learn more interesting facts about space.

- There are nine planets in our **solar system**. They are Mercury, Venus, Earth, Mars, Jupiter, Saturn, Uranus, Neptune, and Pluto.

- Stars are made of burning gases. They produce their own light, and exist in large groups known as galaxies.

- The Sun is a star.

- Many astronauts work at NASA. "NASA" stands for National **Aeronautics** and Space Administration.

- Humans explore space using telescopes, rockets, and **space probes**.

- Some animals have been sent to space for research purposes. Animals in space have included mice, rats, monkeys, dogs, and fish.

Looking Up

Humans have been watching the evening sky for thousands of years. Scientists began using telescopes to learn about the objects in space, such as stars. They learned about the movements, shapes, and colors of space objects. They also learned about the locations and surfaces of the planets. Before long, people wanted to explore space through travel.

■ Some astronomers study space using giant telescopes. California's Palomar Observatory is one such telescope.

First in Space

A human traveled to space for the first time on April 12, 1961. Yuri Gagarin was the first person in space.

Yuri Gagarin was a Russian air force pilot. He was chosen to go on a special mission. Yuri was the first human to fly in space. On April 12, 1961, Yuri **launched** into space in a tiny capsule called *Vostok 1*. He made an **orbit** around Earth at a speed of 17,000 miles (27,359 km) an hour. His trip lasted almost 2 hours.

Moonwalk

NASA sent American astronauts to the Moon in 1969. Americans Neil Armstrong and Buzz Aldrin were the first humans to set foot on the Moon. The astronauts wore protective spacesuits when they stepped onto the Moon's surface. They gathered Moon rocks and brought them back to Earth to be studied.

■ Neil Armstrong took photographs of Buzz Aldrin walking on the Moon.

Moon Talk

Neil Armstrong made an important speech when he visited the Moon. Many people still remember his words.

Did you know that millions of people watched the first moonwalk? They watched the event on television. When Neil Armstrong stepped onto the Moon's surface, he said: "That's one small step for man, one giant leap for mankind." Landing on the Moon was a great advance in space exploration.

Moving to Mars

So far, astronauts have only landed on the Moon. They have not visited any of the planets in our solar system. Mars is the next destination for space explorers. Astronauts will have to wear protective spacesuits when they land on Mars. This is because the planet does not support life. Its atmosphere is too thin.

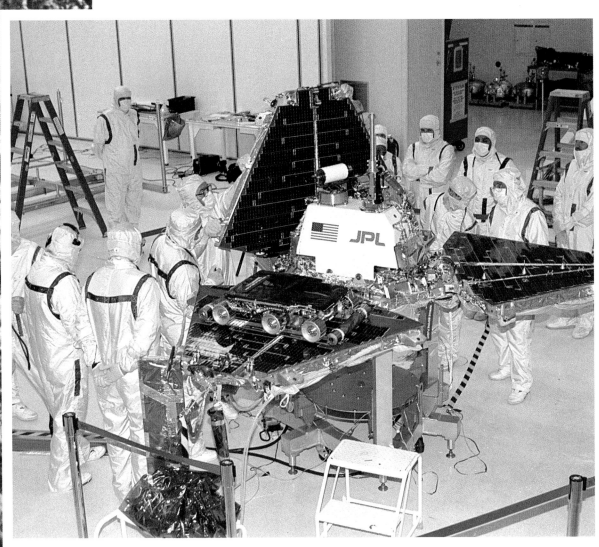

■ *Sojourner* is a moving robot that was built by NASA. It was sent to Mars inside the *Mars Pathfinder*.

A Life of Science

Joy Crisp

Joy Crisp has worked for NASA for many years. She is not an astronaut, but she does explore space. She studies Mars from Earth. NASA sent a **rover** named *Sojourner* to Mars. *Sojourner* was used to test the soil and rocks on Mars. Joy Crisp sent messages to *Sojourner* using a computer. These messages were instructions to move and send images back to Earth.

Solar System Map

Match each planet on the left to its orbit in the diagram. This will show you the order of the planets in our solar system.

- Mercury

- Venus

- Earth

- Mars

- Jupiter

- Saturn

- Uranus

- Neptune

- Pluto

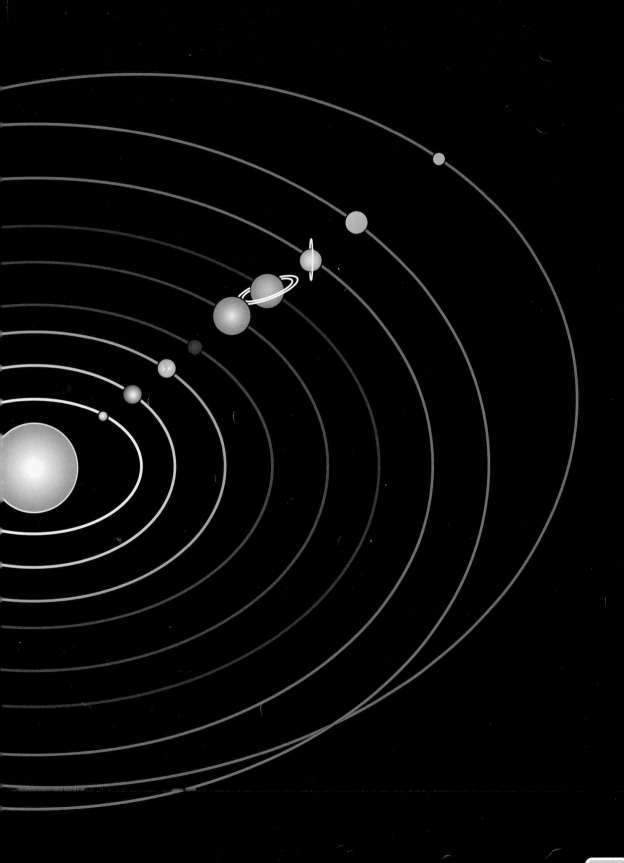

The International Space Station

A large spacecraft has been built to help astronauts carry out space research. It is called the International Space Station. The space station stays in space, orbiting Earth. Scientists use the space station to study Earth and space. They are also learning how humans can live and work in space for long periods of time.

■ The United States and fifteen other countries worked together to build the International Space Station.

Breathing in Space?

Astronauts cannot leave their spacecraft without spacesuits. These protective suits allow astronauts to stay in space for up to 8 hours.

Try to hold your breath for 1 minute. Before long, you will need to take a deep breath of air. A spacesuit supplies astronauts with the oxygen needed to stay alive. A special backpack attached to the spacesuit supplies oxygen. Oxygen tanks can be recharged and used again.

Hubble in Space

Sojourner is not the only machine that helps scientists study space. The *Hubble Space Telescope* allows humans to see distant space objects. It makes space objects appear closer than they are.

The *Hubble Space Telescope* was launched into space on April 24, 1990. Today, it continues to orbit Earth. Hubble takes wonderful photographs of the planets and moons in our solar system.

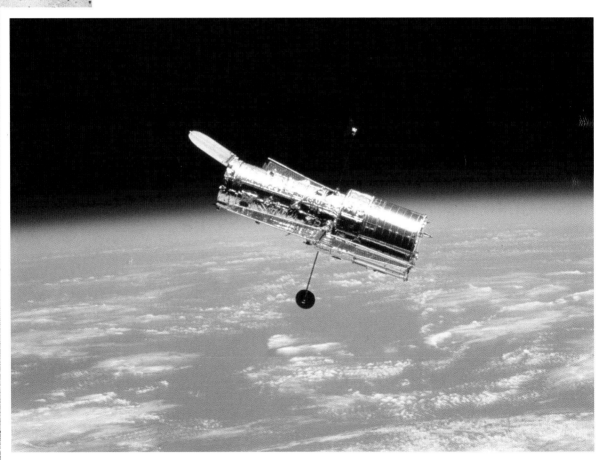

■ Humans have learned much about space from the photographs taken by the *Hubble Space Telescope*.

A Life of Science

Edwin Hubble

Edwin Hubble was born in Missouri in 1889. He loved to read stories about space travelers when he was young.

When Edwin grew up, he became an astronomer. He spent many hours studying the sky using a giant telescope. Edwin made a great scientific discovery with this telescope. He found groups of stars known as galaxies. Edwin Hubble died in 1953. NASA named its large space telescope after Edwin Hubble.

A Future in the Sky

Some astronomers believe that humans will explore other stars someday. Distant stars are similar to our star, the Sun. The stars are very, very far from Earth. Visiting another star would take many years of space travel.

Scientists think there could be other planets similar to Earth in the universe. Such planets might support life if they had air and water. Humans could possibly live on these planets one day.

■ Some galaxies are so far away that humans could never travel to them in a lifetime.

New Astronauts Wanted

New astronauts are always needed for future space exploration. Read on to find out how you can prepare for a life in space.

To become an astronaut, you should work hard at school. Strong mathematics and science skills are important. Success in school is the first step toward becoming a space explorer.

Astronauts also need to exercise. They must stay in good physical shape. Many of them stay strong by swimming, playing soccer, or hiking. Taking part in physical activities will make your body strong and healthy. This is a great way to prepare for a career in space.

Surfing Our Solar System

How can I find more information about space?

- Libraries have many interesting books about space.
- Science centers are great places to learn about space.
- The Internet offers some great Web sites dedicated to space.

Where can I find a good reference Web site to learn more about space?

Encarta Homepage

www.encarta.com

- Type any space-related term into the search engine. Some terms to try include "asteroid " and "galaxy."

How can I find out more about space, rockets, and astronauts?

NASA Kids

http://kids.msfc.nasa.gov

- This Web site offers puzzles and games, along with the latest news on NASA's research.

Science in Action

Make an Astronaut's List

Make a list of all the things you think you would need for a space trip. Next, look at the list provided at the bottom of this page. It includes many of the items necessary for space travel.

How many of the following items were on your list? Why are these items important?

- washcloth
- vitamins
- toothbrush
- toolbox
- toilet paper
- telescope
- storage bags
- spacesuit
- soap
- sleeping bag
- paper
- food and water
- first-aid kit

- equipment
- exercise
- computers

- clothing
- camera and film
- air tanks

What Have You Learned?

1 Can humans breathe in space?

2 How do people see the stars and distant planets?

3 Who was the first person to go into space?

4 Who was the first person to walk on the Moon?

5 What is the next planet that humans plan to visit?

6 How does the temperature on Mars compare to Earth's temperature?

7 Who was NASA's large space telescope named after?

8 Name two key skills that future astronauts should work to improve.

9 What was Edwin Hubble's great discovery?

10 Do all space explorers travel in space?

Words to Know

aeronautics: having to do with aircraft, including spacecraft

asteroids: small, solid objects in space that circle the Sun

launched: sent off into space

orbit: to spin around in a circular path

rover: a robotic vehicle used to explore the surface of a planet

solar system: a group of planets and other bodies that orbit a star

space probes: spacecrafts used to gather information about space

telescope: an instrument that makes distant objects appear closer

universe: everything that exists in space, from dust to large planets

Index